WORLD SOCCER LEGENDS

STARS OF
WOMEN'S
SOCCER

Abbeville Press Publishers
New York · London

A portion of the book's proceeds are donated to the Hugo Bustamante AYSO Playership Fund, a national scholarship program to help ensure that no child misses the chance to play AYSO Soccer. Donations to the fund cover the cost of registration and a uniform for a child in need.

Text by Illugi Jökulsson

For the original edition
Design: THANK YOU
Layout: Árni Torfason

For the English-language edition
Production manager: Louise Kurtz
Layout: Ada Rodriguez
Editor: Sharon Lucas

PHOTOGRAPHY CREDITS

Getty Images: p. 6 (Mike Hewitt - FIFA), 8 (Felipe Oliveira), 10 (Lars Baron - FIFA), 13 (Matthew Stockman), 14 (Maja Hitij), 16 (Kevin C. Cox), 19 (Dennis Grombkowski/Bongarts), 21 (Mitchell Leff), 23 (Jamie Sabau), 24 (Patrick McDermott), 27 (Adam Pretty), 28 (Nils Petter Nilsson/Ombrello), 30 (Hannah Peters), 32 (Michael Regan), 35 (TF-Images), 37 (Eric Verhoeven/Soccrates), 39 (Kevin C. Cox - FIFA), 40 (Kevin C. Cox), 42 (Mike Hewitt - FIFA), 44 (Maja Hitij), 46-47 (Stuart Franklin - FIFA), 48 (Matthew Stockman), 50 (VI Images), 52 (Mike Zarrilli), 58 (Stanley Chou), 60 (Jamie Squire)

AFP: p. 55 (Scanpix Sweden/Bjorn Lindgren)

Bildbyrån: p. 56

First published in the United States of America in 2018 by Abbeville Press, 116 West 23rd Street, New York, NY 10011

First edition
10 9 8 7 6 5 4 3 2 1

Library of Congress Cataloging-in-Publication Data is available upon request.

For bulk and premium sales and for text adoption procedures, write to Customer Service Manager, Abbeville Press, 116 West 23rd Street, New York, NY 10011, or call 1-800-ARTBOOK.

Visit Abbeville Press online at www.abbeville.com.

CONTENTS

BRONZE

ENGLAND

6

LUCY BRONZE
DEFENDER/RIGHT-BACK
ENGLAND
HEIGHT 5'8"

BORN OCTOBER 28, 1991
IN BERWICK-UPON-TWEED, ENGLAND

CURRENT TEAM:
OLYMPIQUE LYON, FRANCE

INTERNATIONAL GAMES: 51
GOALS: 6

When Lucy Bronze was a young girl growing up in northern England, she spent all her time outdoors playing soccer with the kids in her neighborhood. As is often the case with younger age groups, girls and boys play together, and there the boys certainly met their match. While the boys dreamt of one day becoming famous professional soccer players with Manchester United or Liverpool, or on the national team, Lucy was more modest in her aspirations, and wanted to become an accountant. Regarding any fantasies about joining the national team, she simply said: "I didn't even know that was possible." For a while, England lagged behind other countries in women's soccer, but recent years have seen some dramatic progress. Women players still receive much less attention than male players, but the situation is improving, not least by virtue of the talent and determination of players like Lucy Bronze. She increasingly attracted attention for playing as an attacking right-back for Sunderland, Everton, Liverpool, and Manchester City, and in 2017, she joined the famed Lyon team in France. The accountant dreams have been put on hold—for the meantime at least—since she is now considered one of England's top soccer players.

The English national team was considered second-rate for many years, but Bronze's generation helped catapult it to unforeseen heights. At the 2015 World Cup, England landed in third place and Bronze was shortlisted for the Golden Ball, won by Carli Lloyd. Though a defender, Bronze scored two important goals. During the 2017 Euro, the much-lauded English team reached the semifinals. Captain Steph Houghton drove the powerful defense, while Jodie Taylor flourished in the offense and became the top goal scorer. Both Houghton and Taylor were selected for the team of the tournament—along with Lucy Bronze.

GERMANY

DÄBRITZ

8

SARA DÄBRITZ
MIDFIELDER
GERMANY
HEIGHT 5'7"

BORN FEBRUARY 15, 1995
IN AMBERG, BAVARIA, GERMANY

CURRENT TEAM:
BAYERN MÜNCHEN, GERMANY

INTERNATIONAL GAMES: 48
GOALS: 8

Germany's success at the 2016 Olympic Games in Rio de Janeiro, where they took home the gold, was perhaps not that surprising given Germany's knack for assembling winning teams, both men's and women's. However, the team had undergone many changes, and some pundits suspected that Germany's performance might not be as confident as usual. For example, many were skeptical over coach Sylvia Neid's decision to position 21-year-old Sara Däbritz in the midfield. It turned out that Däbritz fully lived up to Neid's expectations.

Her performance was close to immaculate, and the only time Germany lost was in a game where Däbritz sat on the bench. She scored three important goals in the five games she played, and was brimming with confidence the entire time, contributing both to offense and defense, though it is apparent that "Däbritz" prefers shooting and passing to defensive play. The letter "ä" is pronounced with an "e" sound in German. Commit the sound of the name Sara "Debritz" to memory—soccer fans will hear it repeated often in the decade to come.

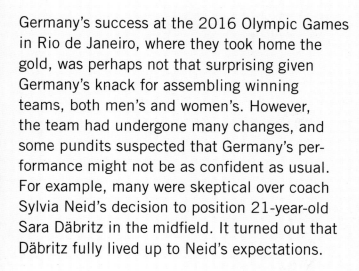

Däbritz was born and raised in the town of Amberg in Bavaria, which is the southernmost and largest state in Germany. Bayern München is by far the most famous team in Bavaria, and is supported by most of the region's residents. The young Däbritz grew up surrounded by loyal Bayern fans, and her deepest wish was to one day join the team. She began her career with Freiburg, but when she turned 20, Bayern finally came knocking. Sara Däbritz is living proof that dreams can indeed come true.

DELIE

FRANCE

MARIE-LAURE DELIE
STRIKER
FRANCE
HEIGHT 5'7.5"

BORN JANUARY 29, 1988
IN VILLIERS-LE-BEL, PARIS, FRANCE

CURRENT TEAM:
PARIS ST. GERMAIN, FRANCE

INTERNATIONAL GAMES: 123
GOALS: 65

Despite the fact that France has acquired a number of fantastic soccer players in the recent years, no one surpasses Marie-Laure Delie when it comes to goal scoring. She is now entered second place on the list of top French goal-scorers of all time, and if she maintains her pace, she might just jump ahead of Marinette Pichon, who scored 81 goals over the years 1994 and 2008. A year after Pichon's retirement, the 21-year-old Delie played her first international game, starting as she meant to continue by scoring a goal in her debut against Croatia.

Delie had at that time just transferred to Montpellier from Paris St. Germain, but returned to Paris in 2013. No matter where she finds herself, Delie hunts for goal-scoring opportunities within the opponents' penalty box, racking up 102 goals in 120 games with Paris. Marie-Laure Delie is a classic striker, one you should never take your eyes off, because she will use every possible chance she gets to blast a deadly shot. Full of ball skills, tricks, and tactics, this sharpshooter always has her eyes firmly fastened on goal.

During the 2015 World Cup, it was unclear whether the famous French team would make it through the group stage—the team had to secure a victory in the last game against Mexico. Delie swept in, and inspired her teammates by scoring a goal after only 34 seconds had elapsed. She went on to score two goals in a 3–0 victory over South Korea during the round of 16, but failed to prevent France's defeat at the hands of Germany in a penalty shootout.

JULIE ERTZ
(FORMERLY JULIE JOHNSTON)
DEFENDER/MIDFIELDER
UNITED STATES
HEIGHT 5'7"

BORN APRIL 6, 1992
IN MESA, AZ, USA

CURRENT TEAM:
CHICAGO RED STARS, IL, USA

INTERNATIONAL GAMES: 57
GOALS: 14

Growing up in Mesa, Arizona, it was clear from early on that Julie Ertz was a talented athlete in the making. She lived and breathed all kinds of sports, and volunteered as a student athletic trainer throughout high school. She played with great distinction for the Santa Clara Broncos, and in 2014, she joined the Chicago Red Stars, where she served as center-back, and was a breakout star in this position for the US during the 2015 World Cup.

Always versatile in her talents, Ertz is currently playing defensive midfielder for both club and country—crushing opposing offenses, playmaking, and scoring goals—and was voted 2017 US Soccer Female Player of the Year in this pivotal role. Ertz is only the third player to have won both this award and the Young Female Player of the Year, which she won in 2012 in recognition of her captaining the US to the U-20 Women's World Cup title, and winning the Bronze Ball as the third-best player in the tournament. And the chances are, there are many more awards to come!

In 2015, the World-Cup-winning national team was honored at the White House, following the team's jubilant 5–2 defeat over Japan. President Obama praised the champions: "This team taught all of America's children that 'playing like a girl' means you're a badass." These words refer not least to the relentless and resilient Julie Ertz—she never gives up, and puts every ounce of her strength into her on-field battles.

ERTZ

UNITED STATES

Danmark - Østrig
Breda
03.08.2017

PERNILLE HARDER
STRIKER
DENMARK
HEIGHT 5'6"

BORN NOVEMBER 15, 1992
IN IKAST, JYLLAND, DENMARK

CURRENT TEAM:
WOLFSBURG, GERMANY

INTERNATIONAL GAMES: 94
GOALS: 50

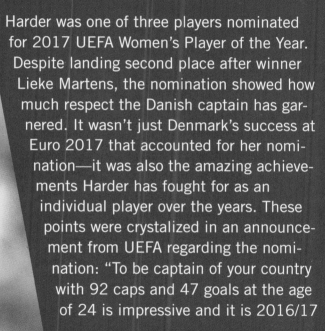

Harder was one of three players nominated for 2017 UEFA Women's Player of the Year. Despite landing second place after winner Lieke Martens, the nomination showed how much respect the Danish captain has garnered. It wasn't just Denmark's success at Euro 2017 that accounted for her nomination—it was also the amazing achievements Harder has fought for as an individual player over the years. These points were crystalized in an announcement from UEFA regarding the nomination: "To be captain of your country with 92 caps and 47 goals at the age of 24 is impressive and it is 2016/17 that has really confirmed Pernille Harder as one of the world's best."

Harder was only 17 years old when she played in her first national game for Denmark. At 20, she transferred to the Swedish team Linköping. It was in the powerful Swedish league that the forward achieved stardom, and scored a goal in almost every game. She then moved to Germany where she joined Wolfsburg and continued her success. Harder's nine goals in 14 games contributed greatly to the team's victory in the Bundesliga and the DFP-Pokal (German Cup), and the 2017 Euro catapulted her to the highest echelon of the world's greatest forwards.

HARDER

Harder is the perfect forward, both strong and agile, determined, and brimming with fighting spirit. Her role in Denmark's recent successes cannot be underestimated.

HEATH

TOBIN HEATH
MIDFIELDER
UNITED STATES
HEIGHT 5'6"

BORN MAY 29, 1988
IN BASKING RIDGE, NJ, USA

CURRENT CLUB:
PORTLAND THORNS. OR, USA

INTERNATIONAL GAMES: 132
GOALS: 18

Despite Tobin Heath's goal-scoring abilities while under great pressure, her central role is to drive the midfield play and create opportunities for her attacking teammates. And she certainly delivers, and then some! She is one of the US's most ingenious midfielders, and her reputation has traveled around the world. When she played with Paris St. Germain 2013–2014, she was the team's best player—an impressive feat, given the fact that there is no lack of legends in the ranks of PSG. Heath is a soccer player to the bone, and when she played with Tar Heels, the University of North Carolina women's team, her teammates claimed that "she would find her way to a soccer field morning, noon, and night."

In 2016, Heath was chosen Soccer Female Player of the Year by the US Soccer Federation. The nomination was phrased in flattering words to say the least: "She has always been one of the USA's most skillful players. She has long dazzled fans with her keen passing and dynamic dribbling, and she creates excitement on whichever flank she happens to occupy, causing nightmares for opposing defenders with her combination of speed, fitness, and soccer savvy."

AMANDINE HENRY, (RIGHT)
DEFENSIVE MIDFIELDER
FRANCE
HEIGHT 5'7"

BORN SEPTEMBER 28, 1989
IN LILLE, FRANCE

CURRENT TEAM:
OLYMPIQUE LYON, FRANCE

INTERNATIONAL GAMES: 69
GOALS: 10

In 2016, US soccer fans got the chance to lay their eyes on one of the legendary players that make up the incredible multi-award-winning French team Lyon. This was Amandine Henry, who is also the new captain of the graceful French national team. Henry joined the Portland Thorns and played there for a season, accompanied by many legends of the US national team that had won the World Cup. And Henry's contributions certainly made a difference. Portland Thorns became champions, and Henry directed the midfield stage like the leader she is. She began her career as a forward and scored countless goals—no wonder given her natural dexterity together with her steady poise and precision aim. Difficult injuries in the beginning of her Lyon days meant that Henry was forced to put the game on hold for a year and a half, and she was close to retiring for good. But she refused to give up, repositioned slightly toward the back, and now plays as a defensive midfielder. Yet she just cannot resist sneaking in a goal from time to time. Following a successful season with Portland Thorns, Henry returned to Europe, and at the beginning of 2018, signed a contract with the team of her roots, Olympique Lyon.

Like many powerful women players, Henry started playing soccer in her youth with the boys. She showed such promise that she was invited to join one of 12 special soccer academies run by the French soccer association around the country. There, talented children are taught techniques that they will build upon as they develop and flourish during their soccer careers. The academies played a large part in strengthening both the French women's and men's national teams.

HENRY

ALI KRIEGER
RIGHT-BACK
UNITED STATES
HEIGHT 5'6"

BORN JULY 28, 1984
IN ALEXANDRIA, VA, USA

CURRENT TEAM:
ORLANDO PRIDE, FL, USA

INTERNATIONAL GAMES: 98
GOALS: 1

Alexandra Krieger's surname is derived from German, and means "warrior," and it is safe to say that the name is a perfect fit. Krieger's father was a soccer coach, and her older brother is also a player. She idolized her brother, which led to her original interest in the sport. And the game seemed well suited to her competitive nature and fighting spirit: In 2005, she fought her way out of a serious illness that could have killed her (blood clots had traveled from her legs to her lungs). She recovered to full health, and following great achievements with Penn State team Nittany Lions, her professional career truly kicked off when she moved to Germany in 2007 and joined FFC Frankfurt. Despite the distance from home base, Krieger's performance attracted the attention of the US coach, who selected her to join the national team in 2008. She played in all of the US's games during the 2011 World Cup in Germany, where the US team landed second place. Krieger suffered a serious injury a year later, but her warrior nature burst through and she battled to full health once again, earning a place on the US national team that became 2015 world champions in Canada. Krieger will no doubt continue to battle for her deserved place in the national team for years to come.

Speaking about herself and her brother, Krieger says: "I think without struggle you can't grow as a person—I think you need that in your life. I have fallen a few times and each time I have gotten up and grown as a person and looked at things a little differently. That is where I have learned so much from Kyle. [Seeing him] struggling through addiction and alcoholism and overcoming that and overcoming adversity, for me that's just an unreal role model in my life."

UNITED STATES

KRIEGER

SYDNEY LEROUX

STRIKER
UNITED STATES
HEIGHT 5'7"

BORN MAY 7, 1990
IN SURREY, BRITISH COLUMBIA, CANADA

CURRENT TEAM:
UTAH ROYALS, UA, USA

INTERNATIONAL GAMES: 77
GOALS: 35

Sydney Leroux was born and raised in Canada to a single Canadian mother. Her American father had left the family shortly after Leroux was born. Both parents were athletes; her father was a baseball player and her mother played softball in Canada. Despite a happy childhood in Canada, Leroux always dreamt of making it big in her father's home country. At the age of 15, she moved to the US and joined UCLA in California. She has resided in the US ever since, with a dual citizenship there and in Canada. Leroux had played with the U-19 team in Canada but when it was her turn to play with the U-20 team in the US, she would inevitably enter the field under an American banner. In 2011, Leroux played her first full international for the US. During the CONCACAF qualifications for the Olympics, Leroux flourished as a striker. In just her second international game Leroux showed that few players would be able to match her in terms of cunning, strength, and finishing, scoring a whopping five goals in a game against Guatemala. The game proved an easy victory for the US, who crushed their opponents 13–0. Leroux remains one of the US's most dangerous strikers, and will doubtlessly continue to rack up goals for many years to come.

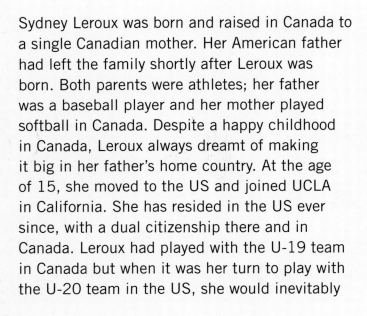

Sydney Leroux is one of the most visible of the US international players. She has appeared on the covers of many magazines: "I think it's a big deal to be an athlete and feel confident in your body and show it off. I'm not going to say I've never struggled with how I look, but I've reached a point in my life where I'm happy with who I am."

LEROUX

LE SOMMER

EUGÉNIE LE SOMMER
FORWARD/ATTACKING MIDFIELDER
FRANCE
HEIGHT 5'3"

BORN MAY 18, 1989
IN GRASSE, RIVIERA, FRANCE

CURRENT TEAM:
OLYMPIQUE LYON, FRANCE

INTERNATIONAL GAMES: 147
GOALS: 63

In the good company of Wendie Renard and midfielders Louisa Nécib and Camille Abily, the forward Eugénie Le Sommer is emblematic of the great advancement and recent successes of both the French league champions Lyon and the magnificent French national team. She was only 19 years old when she played her first game with the national team, and a year later she left Stade Briochin to join the ranks of Lyon. There she has truly blossomed as a well-rounded soccer player and gathered a host of titles, and now it's only a matter of time when the French team snatches the title at a major tournament, either the World Cup or the Euro. Despite Le Sommer's seemingly extensive track record, she is still under 30, and is likely to remain in her place among the world's best for many years to come. Le Sommer's gifts are embodied in her confident ball control, as well as her particular flair for weaving her way through the opponent's defense. In fact, Le Sommer is an all-round player and scores goals of every kind. In 2017, she had played in nearly 240 games and scored 215 goals, almost a goal per game, the statistics of a soccer superstar.

Le Sommer can play both as a striker (a "nine"), a "false nine" or a traditional offensive midfielder, or a "ten". The purpose of the "false nine" is to create problems for the opposing center-backs and/or using the space left open in the pursuit of the "real nine" in order to pass, create opportunities, or shoot.

MELANIE LEUPOLZ
MIDFIELDER
GERMANY
HEIGHT 5'8"

BORN APRIL 14, 1994
IN WANGEN IM ALLGÄU, BAVARIA, GERMANY

CURRENT TEAM:
BAYERN MÜNCHEN, GERMANY

INTERNATIONAL GAMES: 50
GOALS: 8

Melanie Leupolz is one of the most promising German midfielders playing today. Leupolz and Sara Däbritz (see pages 8–9) traveled similar paths in their lives, both growing up in small Bavarian towns (Wangen in Leupolz's case), they played together for Freiburg, went to the same school, and then both joined the German powerhouse Bayern München, one year apart. They have both become stars, and amassed several awards for their performances. What is more, they entered the national team around the same age, played with Germany at the 2015 World Cup in Canada, and together won the gold at the 2016 Summer Olympics in Rio de Janeiro. Leupolz is an incredibly skillful and cunning midfielder and her young age is no hindrance—quite the contrary—and her style is both mature and confident beyond her years. With amazing ball control, she can break free from any tight spot, and then send inch-perfect passes to teammates. The new German team, captained by Maroszán, with Leupolz and Däbritz midfield, Popp up-front and Peter as the defensive bulwark, is sure to put up a good fight and send shivers down the spines of any opponents who meet them on the field. A talented and experienced midfielder like Lena Goeßling will have to make every effort to prove her worth to the national team, such is the upsurge of promising young players like Leupolz.

Leupolz grew up with a kids' soccer field just around the corner from her home. From a young age, she would run to the field the first chance she got and not return home until sundown. Aside from soccer, Leupolz is interested in motorcycles and she has participated in a number of motocross competitions.

LEUPOLZ

LLOYD

CARLI LLOYD
MIDFIELDER/FORWARD
UNITED STATES
HEIGHT 5'7"

BORN JULY 16, 1982
IN DELRAN TOWNSHIP, NJ, USA

CURRENT TEAM:
HOUSTON DASH, TX, USA

INTERNATIONAL GAMES: 246
GOALS: 98

When Carli Lloyd went to the 2015 Women's World Cup in Canada, she was already a veteran of the US national team as attacking midfielder. She was 32 years old, and had participated in nearly 200 international games, scoring in every third game on average. It was therefore obvious that Lloyd would play a vital role in an ambitious team that had set their sights on their third World Cup title. Indeed, she replaced Abby Wambach as made team captain. And even though expectations were high, not even the most hardcore fans could have imagined the kind of performance Lloyd was about to deliver. Already renowned for her work ethic, control, and determination on the field, in Canada she showed her attacking prowess and scoring instincts. Lloyd is famous for scoring important goals, and during the knockout phase she led by example and scored three goals in as many games. In the quarterfinals, she scored the winning goal against the "auld enemy" China. But there was more to come.

Yet, there was more to come: Lloyd's performance in the 2015 World Cup Final against Japan was superlative. She scored the opening goal after only three minutes, and in the sixteenth minute, she bagged a hat trick! The game was essentially over, and ended with a final score of 5–2. After this match, Lloyd entered the realm of US soccer superstars.

DZENIFER MAROZSÁN
MIDFIELDER
GERMANY
HEIGHT 5'7"

BORN APRIL 18, 1992
IN BUDAPEST, HUNGARY

CURRENT TEAM:
OLYMPIQUE LYON, FRANCE

INTERNATIONAL GAMES: 81
GOALS: 32

The German women's national team was near unstoppable over the first decade of the twenty-first century. They won the world championship title both in 2004 and 2007. The magnificent Birgit Prinz covered the frontlines at the time, and the sturdy goalkeeper Nadine Angerer stood guard in the goal. Germany was also invincible in the Euros, with six consecutive tournament victories 1995–2013. After a period of bumpy roads, the German team is now building a fresh team, stronger than ever, and lead by the new captain Dzsenifer Marozsán. The Germans trust that she will steer an exciting team composed of both newcomers and veterans back onto the road of victory. Germany's performance during the 2016 Olympic Games in Rio is a likely indicator of future times ahead, where Marozsán scored one of two goals in Germany's 2–1 victory over Sweden. Marozsán is actually born in Hungary, but moved to Germany at a very young age (her father was a soccer player there). The fact that Marozsán was made captain at such a young age shows that she is a natural-born leader—Germany's previous captains have usually been experienced veterans, but Marozsán's skillfulness in the sport is inarguable. She brilliantly conducts the offense, but she also springs through the defense and racks up countless goals—something spectacular always takes place when Dzenifer Marozsán receives the ball.

MAROZSÁN

In 2017, Marozsán became the youngest player to have played in Germany's top league, the Bundesliga. She was then 14 years and seven months old. She also holds the record as the youngest goal scorer, at the age of 15 years and four months.

BRAZIL

MARTA

MARTA
(FULL NAME MARTA VIEIRA DA SILVA)
ATTACKER
BRAZIL
HEIGHT 5'4"

BORN FEBRUARY 19, 1986
IN DOIS RIACHOS, ALAGOAS, BRAZIL

CURRENT TEAM:
ORLANDO PRIDE, FL, USA

INTERNATIONAL GAMES: 126
GOALS: 113

Marta has resided so long under the spotlight as one of the world's greatest soccer legends that many need a reminder of her age. She is only 32 years old. Many players reach the zenith of their careers at this age, and Martha will no doubt continue to dazzle audiences for many years to come. Marta grew up in a small rural village in central Brazil, but her talents on the field were so conspicuous that the giant team Vasco da Gama, from Rio de Janeiro, invited her to join when she was only 14. Foreign countries soon caught wind of the talented Brazilian, and she set sails on a vast journey and hasn't looked back since. She played for powerful teams in Sweden and the US, as well as in Brazil. At only 20, Marta was awarded the first of five FIFA World Player of the Year titles. In addition, she has amassed countless accolades for her talents and goal-scoring achievements. Marta is like an amalgamation of the Brazilian geniuses Ronaldo and Ronaldinho. She possesses great speed, has a precise aim, and scores goals of every possible variety. And if that wasn't enough, she also has incredible technique, confident ball control and superlative dribbling powers.

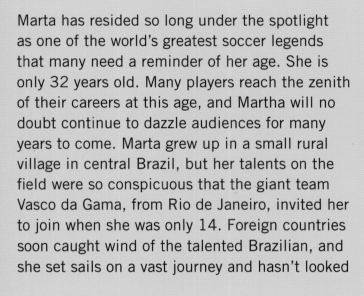

The Brazilian national team counts among the world's greatest, but it has had a bumpy ride at World Cup tournaments. Brazil's best performance was at the 2017 World Cup in Germany, where they were runners-up—mainly due to Marta's genius. She eagerly drove the team, scored seven goals in seven games, and was awarded the Golden Boot.

LIEKE MARTENS
MIDFIELDER
THE NETHERLANDS
HEIGHT 5'7"

BORN DECEMBER 16, 1992
IN BERGEN, NETHERLANDS

CURRENT TEAM:
FC BARCELONA, SPAIN (CATALONIA)

INTERNATIONAL GAMES: 84
GOALS: 33

The Dutch Women's national team played their first game in 1971, and suffered a humiliating defeat at the hands of France. Over the next 40 years, the Dutch team was unfortunately an easy prey for the stronger European teams, and never made it to any major tournament. But then something miraculous happened. Not only did Holland manage to qualify for the 2015 World Cup in Canada and perform there beyond everyone's wildest expectations by fighting their way to the knockout phase, but the team then went on to win the 2017 Euro. The tournament was hosted by Holland, but still no one imagined that the Dutch team would be as strong and triumphant as they turned out to be. The title was absolutely deserved, and their performance was incredible. As the team continues its ascent, two immensely talented and promising women—Vivianne Miedema (see pages 36–37) and Lieke Martens—have emerged on the scene, and are already among the world's best players at the highest level of the game. Martens is only 25 years old but she has played in almost 90 international games, and counting. And she scores a goal in every second and third game on average. She is quick as a whip, highly agile and cunning, and dashes fearlessly into every attack.

The 2017 Euro final was a pure delight to watch. Holland faced Denmark, whose good performance had also come as a surprise when they managed to eliminate the powerful Germans. The Danes scored a goal and were ahead, but Miedema levelled the score, Martens then swept in and scored another goal, giving Holland the lead. The game concluded with Holland's 4–2 victory. Martens received the UEFA Women's Player of the Year award for the 2016/17 season.

MARTENS

VIVIANNE MIEDEMA
STRIKER
THE NETHERLANDS
HEIGHT 5' 9"

BORN JULY 15, 1996
IN HOOGEVEEN, NETHERLANDS

CURRENT TEAM:
ARSENAL, ENGLAND

INTERNATIONAL GAMES: 61
GOALS: 49

The young Vivianne Miedema is an extremely promising forward, bound to be ranked among the world's greatest players ever. She was only 15 years old when she played in her first game with SC Heerenveen, the top league in Holland, and at 17 she played her first international game. It was obvious from the very beginning of Miedema's career that a new soccer genius had sprung upon the world stage, capable of fulfilling every role required of a creative and powerful forward. She was the top goal scorer of the 2015 World Cup qualifications, scoring 15 goals in 13 games—including three hat tricks and all three goals of Holland's victory over Italy, which secured the team a place in the knockout phase. Holland delivered a lackluster performance in the final tournament but managed to compensate at Euro 2017, where the team absolutely flourished as the host nation. There, Miedema fully came into her own and scored against both England and Sweden. In the final, she scored another two goals for Holland in a 4–2 victory over Denmark. "When I get the ball in front of goal I don't overthink things," the clinical forward told FIFA.com. "I know exactly what I need to do."

Miedema is often mentioned in the same breath as her countryman, Arjen Robben. "Yeah, I get that a lot," she once said when the subject was raised. "But Arjen plays very differently to me. It's really cool to be compared to him but, as a woman, it's a bit strange to always be compared to a man. I'm Vivianne Miedema and I don't play like men do."

MIEDEMA

NETHERLANDS

ALEX MORGAN
STRIKER
UNITED STATES
HEIGHT 5'7"

BORN JULY 2, 1989
SAN DIMAS, CA, USA

CURRENT TEAM:
CALIFORNIA GOLDEN BEARS, BERKELEY,
USA

INTERNATIONAL GAMES: 134
GOALS: 80

Alex Morgan is a goal scorer of the highest caliber. She is tremendously versatile, strong, focused, direct, lightning-quick on her feet, and can always find the goal. She is also a team player, and makes an effort to create opportunities, with a keen eye for passes and her teammates' movements on the field. From her youth, it was clear that Morgan would become an outstanding athlete. She was the youngest member of the US national team that landed second place at the 2011 Women's World Cup, where she scored one of two goals in 2–2 draw against Japan. The game went into extra time where the US eventually lost in a penalty shootout. Morgan became an American hero a year later at the Summer Olympics in London. She secured her team a place in the final by scoring the winning goal against Canada in the third minute of extra time. In the final, she made an assist for Carli Lloyd who scored the US's first goal, and then once again contributed to Lloyd's second goal, ensuring the Olympic gold. Morgan played a vital role as part of the fantastic US offense that won the 2015 World Cup in Canada.

Alex Morgan's fame is not limited to majestic performances on the soccer field. She has several advertising contracts, has been featured on numerous magazine covers, and made countless television appearances, all of which have made her one of the US's most familiar soccer celebrities. Morgan has also written a popular book series for a children's and YA audience about kids who earn soccer success through diligence and hard work.

MORGAN

NAGASATO

JAPAN

YUKI NAGASATO
STRIKER
JAPAN
HEIGHT 5'6"

BORN JULY 15, 1987
IN ATSUKI, JAPAN

CURRENT TEAM:
CHICAGO RED STARS, IL, USA

INTERNATIONAL GAMES: 132
GOALS: 58

Yuki Nagasato was only 17 years old when she played her first national game for Japan. She had already attracted attention in her home country for her extreme focus, unrelenting fighting spirt, and fervent appetite for goal scoring. Nagasato, along with other skillful players such as Aya Miyama and Shinobu Ohno, were all emerging as promising soccer players, and joined legendary veteran striker Homare Sawa on the national team. A decade their senior, Sawa had previously found fame with a number of US teams at the beginning of the century. In summer 2011, Nagasato was a member of the Japanese team that surprised everyone by winning the World Cup hosted in Germany. She scored the first goal of the women's campaign, and played in other classic games of the tournament, such as when Japan defeated home-team Germany, and finally played the great fan-favorite US team in the final, which Japan won in penalty shootout on the back of the thrilling extra-time showdown. Four years later, Nagasato (then called Yuki Ogimi) was in the starting lineup as Japan attempted to defend their title. However, the US was hell-bent on revenge, and though Nagasato scored Japan's first goal in the final, the score was already 4–1 to the US, and they secured a decisive victory at 5–2.

Yuki Nagasato stands out from most other top Japanese soccer players, male or female, in that the major part of her career has taken place outside Japan. In 2010, she joined the German team Turbine Potsdam, and has since then played for various European teams, such as Chelsea, Wolfsburg, and Frankfurt. Nagasato's eye for the goal and steely focus is bound to bring success wherever she goes. In 2017, Nagasato moved to Illinois, where she now plays with the Chicago Red Stars.

O'HARA

KELLEY O'HARA
WINGER/FORWARD
UNITED STATES
HEIGHT 5'5"

BORN AUGUST 4, 1988
IN FAYETTEVILLE, GA, USA

CURRENT TEAM:
UTAH ROYALS FC, UT, USA

INTERNATIONAL GAMES: 104
GOALS: 2

Some soccer players are rooted to particular positions on the field to the extent that it would be considered severely unwise to alter the scheme. For example, a national team coach who would make Becky Sauerbrunn a striker and Alex Morgan a center-back should be immediately fired. Some players are however more versatile, and happily assume diverse positions. And few are as adaptable as Kelley O'Hara. She began her career as a fantastic forward for Stanford University, where she amassed 57 goals and 32 assists, both school records at time. In 2012, O'Hara had been attached to the national team as a forward but never managed to find her form or a permanent place on the team—No surprise given the strength of her competitors to the offense lineup. When her teammate Ali Krieger suffered an injury in the run up to the London Olympics, coach Pia Sundhage wondered whether O'Hara would be up for playing one or the other of the far-back position. O'Hara was certainly up to it and played as either left-back or right-back for years. At Sky Blue she was back in offense, and at Utah Royals she is likely to continue her success in this role.

As a child, O'Hara was famous for not liking sleepovers with friends. She usually phoned her dad and made him pick her up when night fell. But as she grew up she began to relish challenges, and eventually decided to head to faraway California for college. As she said goodbye to her family she suddenly looked at her father with dread in her eyes and said: "But what if I like it?"

PETER

BABETT PETER

DEFENDER
GERMANY
HEIGHT 5'7"

BORN MAY 12, 1988
IN OSCHATZ, SAXONY, GERMANY

CURRENT TEAM:
WOLFSBURG, GERMANY

INTERNATIONAL GAMES: 116
GOALS: 8

After Germany's deserved victory at the 2016 Olympic Games in Rio de Janeiro, then-captain Saskia Bartusiak decided to retire. This finally opened a place in the central defense for Babett Peter, even though she had been part of the national team for a whole decade. Peter has since then become an irreplaceable part of Germany's unyielding defense. At a young age, Peter was given the nickname "Hulk." The reason is not down to physical bulk nor is due to ferocity on the field, it is rather because she is absolutely unwavering and sturdy on her feet. No forward should dare to unsettle Peter's balance or attempt to knock her down. Her defensive strategy and intelligence in reading the game makes dribbling past her almost impossible. The German Bundesliga is an enduring institution of such strength that women players rarely transfer to foreign leagues. And Peter has only played in Germany up until this point. She became German champion five times with Turbine Potsdam, as well as the Women's Championship League title, and the German Cup. Peter won the German Cup again with FFC Frankfurt, 2012–2014, and then transferred to Wolfsburg with whom she has won the Cup three times and one Bundesliga title.

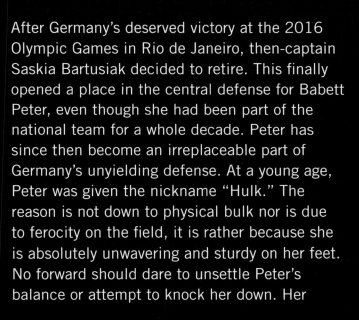

Peter has suffered from facial-nerve paralysis since the age of five. The condition has in no way stopped her from flourishing as a soccer player, and she has met her disease with the same diligence and resolve with which she tackles her opponents on the field.

ALEXANDRA POPP

FORWARD/ATTACKING MIDFIELDER
GERMANY
HEIGHT 5'9"

BORN APRIL 6, 1991
IN WITTEN, NORTH RHINE-WESTPHALIA, GERMANY

CURRENT TEAM:
WOLFSBURG, GERMANY

INTERNATIONAL GAMES: 83
GOALS: 40

Two of the greatest goal scorers in Germany's powerful national team both retired in the period 2015–2017, namely, Celia Sasic and Anja Mittag. It became clear that even more responsibility would fall on Alexandra Popp's shoulders. Popp has played for the national team since 2010, debuting at only 19 years old, to great success. So now the pressure is on Popp to rack up the goals on behalf of the team, which is fortunate for Germany, because Popp is clearly reaching the zenith of her soccer career as the goal-scoring machine that she is. Popp first entered the world stage when she played for the U-20 German national team at the 2010 World Cup. Germany won the tournament with a marvelous team, in which Dzenifer Marozsán burst forth as a fully rounded player, but no one performed better than Popp. She scored in every game, with a total of 10 goals in six games. Popp has amassed a host of accolades with her team Wolfsburg in the Bundesliga, becoming league champion three times, and winning the Champions League title twice. Germany's siege on the US's current World Cup title in 2019 will largely depend on the performance of this versatile and dynamic forward. There is no lack of will: "I want to give absolutely everything I can for the team!"

Despite Popp's young age, and a bright future as one of the world's top players, she has already begun to prepare for life beyond soccer. Popp is a trained zookeeper and works at a zoo in the town of Lehre: "All the animals we have are special. I like working with animals. You can have a connection with kangaroos, to raccoons, or donkeys."

POPP

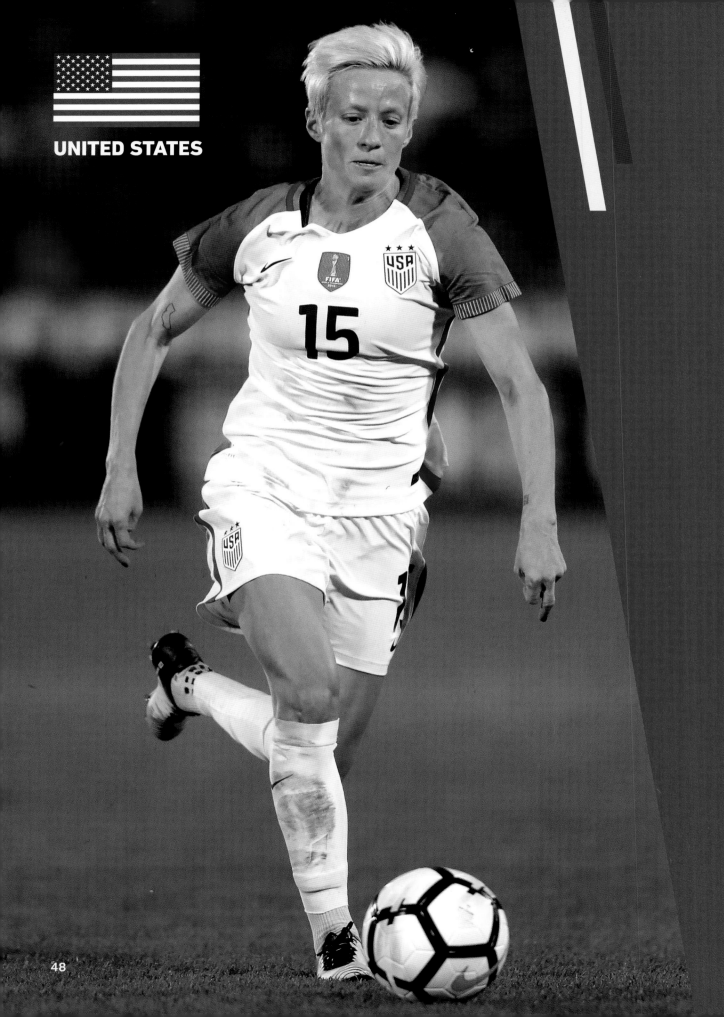

MEGAN RAPINOE
MIDFIELDER/WINGER
UNITED STATES
HEIGHT 5'6"

BORN JULY 5, 1985
IN REDDING, CA, USA

CURRENT TEAM:
SEATTLE REIGN FC, WA, USA

INTERNATIONAL GAMES: 129
GOALS: 34

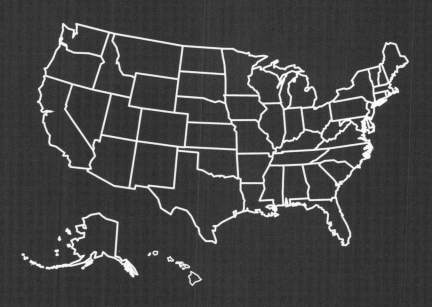

The blond-haired and soaring Rapinoe is a symbol of the dynamic US national team in the beginning of the twenty-first century. As a young girl in her hometown of Redding (population 90,000) north of Sacramento, she enjoyed playing a variety of sports, from track and field to basketball, but soccer was what she excelled at, and became her central passion. As a teenager she commuted two and a half hours from her home to play for Elk Grove Pride in the neighboring city. She was a big hit with the Portland university team, and was consequentially transferred to the Chicago Red Stars. She has traveled far and wide since then, playing in Australia, and joining Lyon in France. Since 2013, Rapinoe has played for Seattle Reign. Rapinoe made her international debut in 2006. However, a serious injury prevented her from obtaining a permanent place on the national team. About her injuries, she said that "getting hurt was one of the best things that ever happened to me. It really gave me a different perspective. Before, everything was going how it was supposed to and I wasn't really appreciative of what I was doing and what it took to get there." From 2009, Rapinoe has been almost omnipresent on the field, though mostly as a combative yet always graceful left-winger.

RAPINOE

Rapinoe has for years been an outspoken advocate for LGBT rights in the US: "To truly express yourself, you have to face who you are and never hide."

RENARD

WENDIE RENARD
CENTER-BACK
FRANCE
HEIGHT 6'1"

BORN JULY 20, 1990
IN SCHOELCHER, MARTINIQUE, FRANCE

CURRENT TEAM:
OLYMPIQUE LYON, FRANCE

INTERNATIONAL GAMES: 98
GOALS: 19

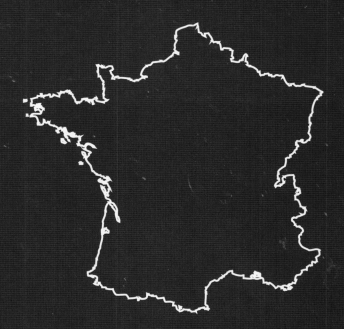

Around 2010, the French women's national team took a sudden leap forward. One day a lackluster mid-range European team, the next they had undergone a complete transformation, becoming one of Europe's strongest teams. The reason for these changes can be traced to the emergence of a new generation of extremely talented individuals, who managed to band together, create a common bond, and form a holistic team. A key figure in this total metamorphosis is the imposing yet technically gifted Wendie Renard, team captain. Renard hails from the Caribbean island Martinique, which has been under French control since colonial times. At only 15 years old, Renard was transferred to French team Lyon. In 2017, Renard had amassed 11 French league titles with the team, as well as winning seven cups, and the Women's Championship League four times. And during this whole time, the powerful center-back served as team captain. At just 21 she debuted for the national team, and was then made to "captain only two years later—proving her highly impressive leadership skills. However, Amandine Henry has now taken the helm as team captain. Renard and Laura Georges have teamed up in the defenses for both Lyon and the national team, though Georges now plays for Paris St. Germain.

Along with conducting the defense, Renard is also known for scoring goals. In the end of 2017, she had played almost 300 games with Lyon, and scored 83 times. She has also racked up goals for the national team. Renard's height is an advantage when it comes to free kicks and corner kicks, but she is also a gifted shot—a true penalty-box danger for any defending opponent.

SAUERBRUNN

BECKY SAUERBRUNN
DEFENDER
UNITED STATES
HEIGHT 5' 7"

BORN JUNE 6, 1985
IN ST. LOUIS, MO, USA

CURRENT TEAM:
UTAH ROYALS, UT, USA

INTERNATIONAL GAMES: 135
GOALS: 0

The US national team has always been well-equipped with strong defenders. Center-backs such as Carla Overbeck and Joy Fawcett made a great splash with the US team that conquered the 1999 World Cup. They both served as team captains, each for a few years. No one has held that position over a longer period than Christie Pierce, then known as Christie Rampone, who captained the team 2009–2015. And her inspirational fighting spirit was no less an asset for the national team than Abby Wambach's goals. Two captains were required to fill Pierce's shoes when she retired—Carli Lloyd and Pierce's heir in the defense, Becky Sauerbrunn. The Missouri midfielder is not one to stir up a ruckus. Rather, Sauerbrunn carries out her defensive role with minimum fuss, but she is both quick and effective when called to action. It took Sauerbrunn time to adjust to her position with the national team, and serves as an example of how determination and endurance pays off in sports. She made her international debut in 2008, but performed unevenly in the first years. When the US won gold at the 2012 Olympics in London, she was reserve and spent little time on the field. The turning point was the 2015 World Cup, where she played in all seven games, and had significant impact on the US's achievements at the tournament. Sauerbrunn is only 32 years old. And in light of the fact that Pierce played into her forties, Sauerbrunn will enjoy a long, successful career for many more years.

Sauerbrunn has played for the US 135 times, but has, as this is written, never scored an international goal. This is by no means her purpose in the team. True center-backs often choose to keep clean sheets rather than endangering the team by chasing after goal-scoring opportunities.

LOTTA SCHELIN (FAR RIGHT)
STRIKER
SWEDEN
HEIGHT 5'10"

BORN FEBRUARY 27, 1984
IN TRÅNGSUND, SWEDEN

CURRENT TEAM:
FC ROSENGÅRD, MALMÖ, SWEDEN

INTERNATIONAL GAMES: 185
GOALS: 88

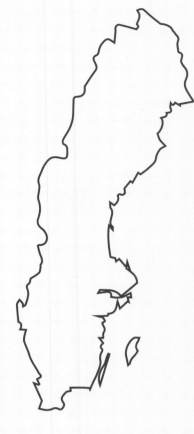

Lotta Schelin is one of the greatest forwards to have ever graced women's soccer. She began her career in 2001 with the Swedish team Göteborg FC, with whom she remained for seven years before joining the famous Lyon in France, where she gathered every kind of accolade. In 2016, Schelin returned to Sweden with 18 cups in her suitcase. At Lyon, she managed the amazing feat of scoring 218 goals in 213 games with the French team. She had just turned 20 when she made her debut with the national team, and has since then delivered consistent performances for her country, though failing to reach the same goal-scoring heights as she had become famous for with Lyon. In 2012, the new coach Pia Sundhage decided that Schelin should share the position of captain with Caroline Seger, an arrangement which has been kept until this day. Both are still in top form, and Schelin's scoring rate is on par with younger forwards. Schelin has been selected Sweden's top player five times, a women's soccer record in her country.

Schelin is tall and strong, and truly a force to be reckoned with in the opponent's penalty box. But she is best known for her long sprints across the field. Speaking about her personal style, she says: "I like to drop deep or go wide in order to find space. . . . I always think of the collective because the danger can come from all players. Even if I do not score, I pass, I run to attract defenders. In the end, I want to win."

SCHELIN

SEGER

SWEDEN

CAROLINE SEGER (LEFT)
MIDFIELDER
SWEDEN
HEIGHT 5'8"

BORN MARCH 19, 1985
IN HELSINGBORG, SWEDEN

CURRENT TEAM:
FC ROSENGÅRD, MALMÖ, SWEDEN

INTERNATIONAL GAMES: 163
GOALS: 23

The Scandinavian countries surged to the top of women's soccer in the 1970s, around the time when it was first gaining proper recognition as a sport, and they have remained at the forefront of the game ever since. When the US won the first women's World Cup in 1995, the team defeated Norway in the final and Sweden landed third place. The Norwegians claimed the world championship title four years later. Swedes were the runners-up at the 2003 World Cup held in the US, and then came third at the 2011 World Cup. Sweden, Norwegians, and Danes have shared the second place between them at recent Euro tournaments. Caroline Seger is the embodiment of the perfect Swedish soccer player. She is diligent and dexterous, teeming with fighting spirit and the ultimate box-to-box midfielder—she is equally at home in both penalty boxes— one moment defending, and the next, deep inside the opponent's defense, honing her aim. Seger has traveled widely over her extensive career—she played in the US 2010–2011 for Philadelphia Independence and later Western New York Flash. She then went on to join the powerful Paris St. Germain and Lyon, both in France, but returned home to Sweden in 2017.

In response to being appointed to the Order of Canada in 2017, which recognizes achievement, dedication, and service to the nation, Sinclair was characteristically humble: "I can dream of winning a World Cup or an Olympic gold medal, and that's my job, but to have your country recognize you—I don't even know what to say."

SINCLAIR

CHRISTINE SINCLAIR
STRIKER/ATTACKING MIDFIELDER
CANADA
HEIGHT 5'9"

BORN JUNE 12, 1983
IN BURNABY, BRITISH COLUMBIA, CANADA

CURRENT TEAM:
PORTLAND THORNS

INTERNATIONAL GAMES: 262
GOALS: 169

Sinclair is captain of the powerful Canadian national team, and she is the main reason for the team's successes over the last 15 years. She is the true talisman for Canada, and the greatest goal scorer that the women's national team has ever possessed, netting goals of every possible type. Sinclair is a truly versatile player, capable of shooting with both feet, and along with scoring goals herself, creates opportunities for teammates with precision passes and brilliant playmaking. Asked about Sinclair in a 2014 interview with CBC, the US goalkeeper Hope Solo was highly complimentary: "I've said for a long time that I believe, in my humble opinion, that Christine Sinclair is the best player in the world. . . . You don't always get to see how brilliant she is because she doesn't always have the support players, but I think now she's starting to get the support players she needs to really highlight her own play." During the 2015 World Cup in Canada, the home team exceeded expectations by making it all the way to the semifinals, where they lost by a hair to the stalwart English team. The BBC raved about Sinclair as a captain who leads by example and inspires her teammates, saying that she was "universally respected by opponents and boasts an international strike rate few can match. Modest and unassuming off the field, Sinclair's drive and passion are hallmarks of her on-field persona."

In response to being appointed to the Order of Canada in 2017, which recognizes achievement, dedication, and service to the nation, Sinclair was characteristically humble: "I can dream of winning a World Cup or an Olympic gold medal, and that's my job, but to have your country recognize you—I don't even know what to say."

SOLO